Kid and the Sticky Skyscraper

Stephen Elboz

Illustrated by Judy Brown

OXFORD

Chapter 1

Kid Wonder and Grandpa were behind bars at Baggem City Prison.

No, they hadn't been arrested. Kid Wonder was a superhero who only fought on the side of law and order. Grandpa was a retired superhero.

They were at the prison visiting Governor Turnkey.

Grandpa and the Governor liked to talk about the good old days of crime-fighting. Kid Wonder was happy just to listen, drinking tea from a big prison mug.

The Governor's office had a window which overlooked the prison yard. Suddenly something caught Kid Wonder's eye.

'Look!' she cried, nearly dropping her mug. 'Isn't that the Slippery Shadow and his gang?' It was hard to recognize them in their prison uniforms.

Governor Turnkey swelled with pride. 'Yes, that's the Slippery Shadow and his gang, hurrying off to their classes.'

'Classes?' said Grandpa. 'Aren't they a bit old to go to school? Heh-heh-heh.'

Governor Turnkey explained that the Shadow and his gang were going to special prison classes. The Slippery Shadow and Baby-face Brewster were learning how to cook.

Fingers O'Brien and Squeaky Malloy were doing extremely well at their building lessons.

'I don't like to boast,' said the Governor. 'But I truly do believe I have made the Slippery Shadow and his men reform. They've become good.'

This time Kid Wonder really *did* drop her mug.

After they had cleared up the mess, Kid Wonder and Grandpa said their goodbyes to the Governor. Kid Wonder picked up Grandpa and flew him back to Haddit House, home for retired superheroes.

Kid Wonder frowned. 'Do you think the Slippery Shadow has turned honest at last, Grandpa?'

'It's kind of hard to believe,' said Grandpa, 'after all his years of crime.'

Chapter 2

Meanwhile, at Baggem City Prison, the Slippery Shadow and his gang couldn't have behaved better.

In fact they were so well behaved that the Governor decided to let them out of prison.

'Tomorrow,' said the Governor, 'you shall be set free!'

'Oh, thank you so much,' said the gang politely. 'But don't go to any trouble just for us.'

The next morning, Police Chief McGrabbem came from City Hall to make a speech. It was so long and boring that Governor Turnkey soon fell asleep.

But the Slippery Shadow and his gang listened politely to every word. They didn't snigger or blow raspberries and at the end they clapped and cheered.

There were tears of joy in the eyes of Governor Turnkey and Police Chief McGrabbem as the prison's heavy metal doors were unlocked.

Nobody saw the Slippery Shadow and his gang grin at each other as they walked away.

Chapter 3

Kid Wonder flew over Baggem City.
She was bored.

The Slippery Shadow and his gang
had been out of prison for a month
and they hadn't broken a single law.
Kid Wonder knew ... she had been
watching them.

'I think I'll go and check up on
them,' she said. 'After all, you can't be
too careful. I might just catch one of
them watching TV without a licence.'

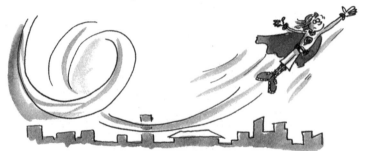

She swooped down on the south side of the city. A new sign had appeared amongst the factories and old work yards.

The Slippery Shadow saw
her looking at his sign.

'Ah, Kid Wonder, what an
honour that you have come
to visit us,' he said smiling.
'Isn't it, boys?'

'Yes, Boss, an honour,'
said the gang, smiling
their most dazzling smiles.

Kid Wonder nodded at the sign.

'So you're making building blocks these days?' she said. She was disappointed. It seemed a perfectly lawful thing to do. 'I suppose,' she went on, 'you learned to make them at your prison classes?'

Squeaky Malloy nodded his head. 'Our building blocks are the best you can buy,' he said. 'They're using them at Trumpet Tower,' added Fingers O'Brien.

Kid Wonder had heard of Trumpet Tower. It was a skyscraper being built by Donald Trumpet, one of the richest men in Baggem City. Only the very rich would be able to afford to live there.

Kid Wonder decided to watch the tower closely. After all, she had nothing else to do.

Chapter 4

Trumpet Tower already rose high over Baggem City. Or rather, its metal girders did. The girders were like the bones of the building, and the blocks that the Slippery Shadow and his gang were busy making were going to be its walls.

Kid Wonder watched.

Each day she saw the gang delivering blocks. Each day she saw the walls of the tower grow a little higher.

Grandpa read the news to Kid Wonder.

'If the Slippery Shadow is going back to his bad ways, it will be today, Grandpa,' said Kid Wonder.

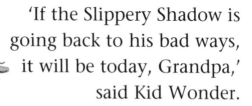

He's sure to have itchy fingers with so many millionaires, billionaires and zillionaires in one place.

'I'd better keep a hold on my pension book,' chuckled Grandpa.

Kid Wonder decided to call Police Chief McGrabbem on her wonderphone. She told him to put all his men around Trumpet Tower, just to be on the safe side.

This is what he did …

The Slippery Shadow and his gang were surrounded by police.

They looked hurt. 'What's the matter, Kid Wonder? Don't you trust us?' shouted the Slippery Shadow.

Baby-face Brewster burst into tears and Squeaky Malloy had to give him his dummy to calm him down.

For once Kid Wonder felt a little sorry for them.

A few minutes later, cars as long as the street began to pull up at the tower's main door. The rich and the famous were coming to live at Trumpet Tower.

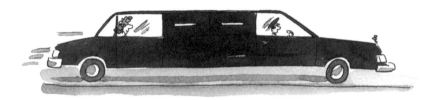

'Keep the crowds under control!' ordered Police Chief McGrabbem.

But there weren't any crowds. The pavement was swarming with too many police!

Just then, Donald Trumpet stepped
beaming from his tower.

A duchess tapped
him on the shoulder.
On her finger gleamed
a big, fat diamond ring.

My man, have you
built me a special
room for my
darling jewels?

'Everything is as I promised,' said Mr
Trumpet, bowing low.

'Hey, are my bath taps solid gold?' demanded Maximillian Bucks the film star.

'The purest and the finest,' answered Mr Trumpet.

'And have you put in special mirrors that make people look taller?' asked a rather short, nervous millionaire.

'Ones that make you look like a giant,' smiled Mr Trumpet.

'Honestly, these rich folks are so-o fussy,' said Grandpa in a loud voice.

'Shh!' hissed Kid Wonder, embarrassed.

23

As more and more rich people arrived and went into the tower, Kid Wonder kept a close watch on the Slippery Shadow and his gang. Would the sight of so much wealth lead them back to a life of crime?

But the Slippery Shadow and his gang simply stood in a sulky silence.

'Do you think, Grandpa, I've been wrong about them all along?' whispered Kid Wonder.

'Perhaps,' said Grandpa. 'Now let's go home. Brrr! It's getting chilly.'

Chapter 5

When they reached Haddit House,
Kid Wonder helped Grandpa into his
favourite cardigan.

'You know, Grandpa,
there's something I
don't understand,' she
said. 'When the
Slippery Shadow and
his gang were in prison,
some of them took
cookery lessons. Now
they're free, they're not
interested in cookery
one little bit. I wonder
why?'

'Haven't a clue,' said Grandpa. 'Now
turn on the fire, dear. There's a cold
wind tonight.'

A cold wind did
indeed blow through
Baggem City. Inside
Trumpet Tower, the
central heating
was turned up full.

As the skyscraper
grew hotter and
hotter, a strange
thing began to
happen.

It started to melt!

Down at City Hall, all was quiet. In fact, it was always quiet these days since the Slippery Shadow and his gang had become honest.

Then in a forgotten corner of the Police Department, a telephone began to ring. Seconds later another started up. Then another and another …

Pretty soon all the telephones were ringing away like mad.

Police Chief McGrabbem ran round doing his best to answer them. Every time he did, the caller shouted the same thing –

Help! Trumpet Tower is melting!

WEEEEEE E

WAA

WEEEEEE

WEEEEEE

WEEEEEE

The Police Chief
immediately sent
twenty squad cars
racing to the scene.
But as soon as the cars
reached the tower,
they skidded into
an oozy river
of sticky goo.

GLUB

At once they were stuck.

28

The police jumped out of their cars, only to end up covered in goo too. As the goo cooled, it set hard.

Baggem City Police Force had turned into living statues.

This was the moment four sniggering figures chose to come creeping out of a doorway.

Who else ... but the Slippery Shadow and his gang!

The police grunted and groaned, but they could not move a finger.

Stick around, boys!

By this time, the walls of Trumpet Tower had melted clean away. The Slippery Shadow and his gang were able to go wherever they liked and steal whatever they pleased.

The reason *they* didn't stick to the goo –

each one of the gang was wearing non-stick saucepans, tied to his feet with string.

At last, with their sacks full of loot, the gang clattered down the street and made a clean getaway.

Chapter 6

As she flew home from Haddit House, Kid Wonder still felt uneasy. She decided to pay Trumpet Tower another visit.

Travelling at the speed of lightning, she dived through a cloud and then almost fell out of the sky in surprise.

In front of her, in the cold moonlight, Trumpet Tower looked like a melted candle.

Kid Wonder needed to know more.

She hovered over one of the melted walls. It had turned hard again, but smelt sweet and strangely familiar. She decided to risk a little lick.

Her tongue told her at once what she was tasting –

The walls had been made of solid blocks of toffee. No wonder they had melted when the central heating had been turned on.

Kid Wonder narrowed her eyes. This could only be the work of the Slippery Shadow and his gang. At last she understood why the Shadow and Baby-face Brewster had been so keen to learn cookery.

My, but the toffee did taste good! Before she knew it, Kid Wonder had licked a hole in it big enough to poke her head through.

'Wait a minute – what am I doing?' she cried. 'I'm a superhero. Crime-fighting must always come first … Well, a couple more licks won't hurt …'

Reluctantly Kid Wonder flew up into the air. Time to track down the Slippery Shadow and his gang and bring them to justice.

'Hey! What about us?' shouted the stuck-solid police force.

Kid Wonder flew up and over the rooftops. Even with her super vision, she knew she was going to have a hard job finding the gang. The Slippery Shadow and his gang would sneak down the darkest alleys and crawl along the smelliest drains, just to escape her.

Then Kid Wonder heard something and smiled.

CLANK - CLANK - CLANK. CLANK

The saucepans had helped the gang to walk over sticky toffee, but on hard concrete you could hear them a mile off.

Kid Wonder's smile grew wider. She had thought of a plan.

Chapter 7

Kid Wonder dived down to Big Joe's All-night Corner Store. She zoomed up to the sweet counter.

Big Joe stood with his arms folded. 'Now then, Kid Wonder. You know what your Grandpa says about eating too many sweets.'

'It's an emergency,' cried Kid Wonder. 'I need it to fight crime.'

Big Joe smiled. 'Oh, really?' he said. 'Has Batman ever needed a chocolate bar to biff his enemies? Or Superman come out on top with a sherbert dab?'

Kid Wonder promised him she was telling the truth. Big Joe sighed. He handed her seventy-five packets of bubblegum.

'Thanks, Joe,' called Kid Wonder as she bounded through the door.

Outside, the moon had gone behind a cloud. But even without its soft, silvery light, she soon caught up with the Slippery Shadow and his gang.

As fast as she could, Kid Wonder unwrapped the bubblegum. She tossed it into her mouth.

Then her jaws went up and down at an amazing speed. She chewed and she chewed and she chewed and she chewed. She chewed until her jaw ached and her ears waggled.

When the chewing was done, she began to blow the world's biggest bubblegum bubble.

It took all of her superhuman strength to blow it up and then stop the wind blowing her away with it.

With one last effort, she took aim and blew the bubble as hard as she could (and for a superhero that *was* hard).

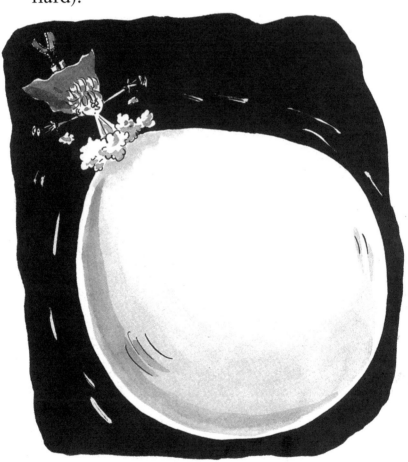

The bubble went speeding away.

The Slippery Shadow and his gang
were captured inside. No matter how
hard they pushed, kicked, bit and
jumped, they could not get out.

The Slippery Shadow gnashed his teeth.

Baby-face Brewster began to cry.

'Aw, shut up!' snapped the rest of the gang bad-temperedly.

Baby-face Brewster sucked his thumb instead.

'Now let's get you villains back to prison where you belong,' said Kid Wonder.

She had no trouble rolling the bubble in front of her.

A special welcome was waiting for them at the prison gates.

The Slippery Shadow gave a sly smile. 'Just how are you going to get us out of here?' he sneered, poking the sides of the bubble.

'Easy,' said Kid Wonder, pulling something from her wonderbelt.

'With *this* –'

'No – no! Mercy!' begged the gang.
But the pin's point flashed as it went
into the bubble and –

out fell the Slippery Shadow and his
gang.

The Governor's men grabbed them
by their collars and marched them
away.

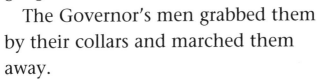

We'll be back!

Chapter 8

For the next few days Kid Wonder had lots to do.

This time she made sure Trumpet Tower was built properly – with blocks of concrete, not toffee.

Mr Trumpet and his rich friends were delighted to get their homes back, as well as all their stolen things.

As for the melted toffee that blocked the roads, Kid Wonder suddenly found she had lots and lots of willing helpers.

THE BAGGEM GLOBE

SCHOOLS CLOSE!

MYSTERIOUS SHORTA OF CHILDR

When everything in Baggem City was back to normal again, Kid Wonder and Grandpa went to visit Governor Turnkey at the City Prison.

How's the Slippery Shadow and his gang?

'Just splendid,' said the Governor. 'Why, only this morning, Baby-face Brewster came from his cookery class and gave me a present –'

He took out a cake from his desk drawer.

Would you like a piece?

Dearest Governor

Kid Wonder stared hard at the cake using her X-ray vision.

'Don't cut it, Governor!' she shouted.

Too late!

'I don't think I will have a slice after all,' said Grandpa, wiping icing off the top of his bald head.

The Governor flew into a cake-covered rage.

That Slippery Shadow and his gang—I don't think any of them will ever turn out good!

This set Kid Wonder thinking ...

Later on, as Kid Wonder drank a cup of cocoa at Haddit House, she asked Grandpa a serious question.

Grandpa thought about this in his usual Grandpa kind of way.

'Yes,' he said at last. 'But only if it's getting better from the measles! Heh-heh-heh!'

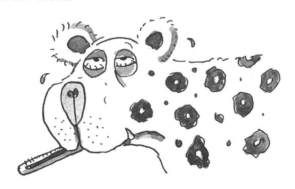

About the author

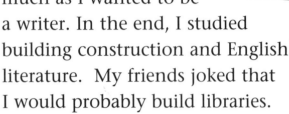

At school I was interested
in becoming an architect
(a person who designs
buildings) almost as
much as I wanted to be
a writer. In the end, I studied
building construction and English
literature. My friends joked that
I would probably build libraries.

But it's a good job I stuck to writing
stories. Any building I designed might
have looked wonderful, but I'm sure
it would have fallen down in ten
minutes flat... just like the sticky
skyscraper in fact.